Learning Toget

For Amelia

my first manual alphabet

FINGERSPELLING

Talking with your fingers
Listening with your eyes
If you think you cannot do it
You're in for a big surprise
With this A B C book
Quite different from the rest
You may find that talking fingers
Are the ones you like the best.

Clare and Carl
arranged and illustrated
by Dorothy and Jacqui Dowling
copyright©
Note: Regional variations in signing may mean
that some signs will differ slightly from the ones
in your own area.
The Standard Manual Alphab

INTRODUCTION

Sign language is a beautiful and expressive way of communication, intriguing for both children and adults. A necessity for the deaf.

Deafness is a very isolating handicap.

This book is specifically designed to assist in the integration and education of both deaf and hearing children in the use of signs and fingerspelling. With fingerspelling alone, you can communicate with any deaf person who uses signing as their only means of communication. Learning the signed alphabet together with the written-spoken one, both deaf and hearing children can learn side by side. In hearing schools, it will be creating an awareness of how deaf people listen with their eyes, and prove of great value in the future. It should be very helpful with topics on hands and hearing, also the need for clear speech to assist with lip-reading.

The aim is to break down the barrier that sadly exists between the deaf and the hearing, an unnecessary barrier. And starting at Nursery and First school age, it should lead on naturally towards this aim.

Anyone wishing to gain more knowledge of signing should get in touch with the local Community Services, Deaf Clubs or Colleges, many of which have sign language classes, or courses for ''communicating with deaf people''.

With this book, it is hoped to arouse in young children, an interest, awareness, and a desire to learn more as they grow up, thus creating better understanding between both groups, and therefore deaf/hearing integration will become a reality.

We hope you enjoy learning your ABC's this way, and have fun with the fingerspelling.

Dorothy and Jacqui

Special thanks to the following for all their help and advice:

Betty Bates	Teacher
Breakthrough Trust	Deaf/Hearing Integration
Roy Bury	Sheffield Lions Club
Barry Cummings	Woodcock Travel, Sheffield
Deaf Advice Service, Sheffield	DASS
Loraine Fletcher	Teacher, Author of ''A Language for Ben''
Paul Fountain	Family and Community Service, Sheffield
Graham Moore	Westfield Health, Sheffield
Sheffield Central Deaf Club	SCDC
James Somerset	SCDC. Now at Derby

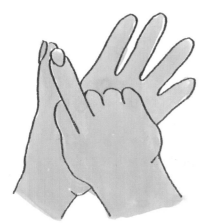 

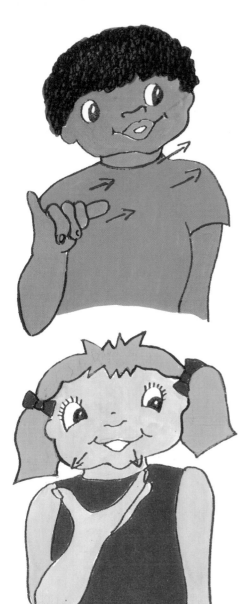

aeroplane

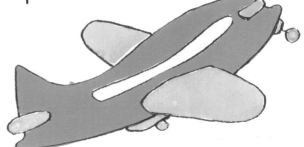

apple

boat

baby

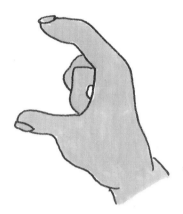

Cc

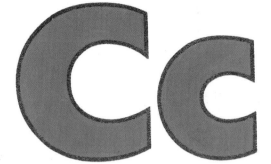

car

cow

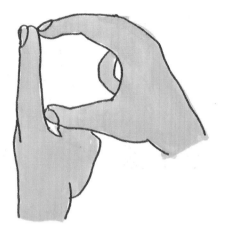 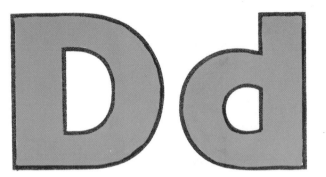

dog

duck

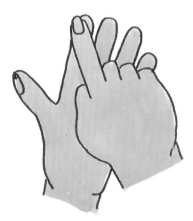

E e

elephant

egg

F f

fish

flowers

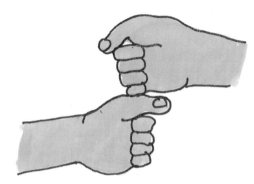

girl

giraffe

Hh

house

helicopter

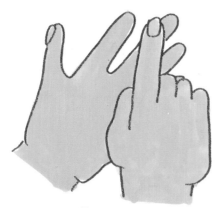

indian

ice cream

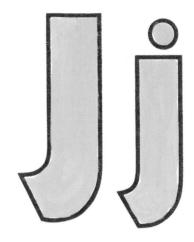

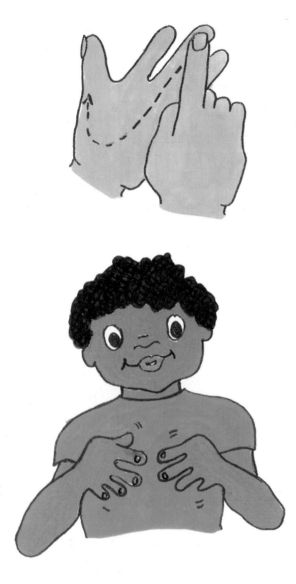

jelly

jumper

king

key

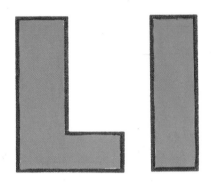

little

large

Mm

mouse

monkey

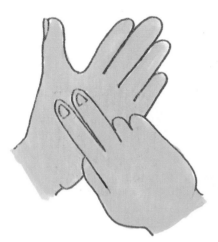

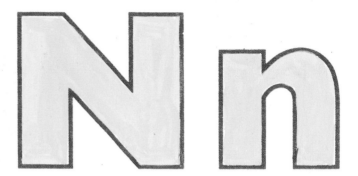

nuts

necklace

 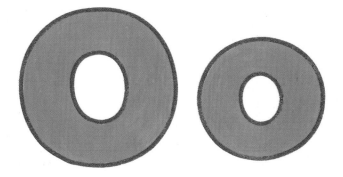

owl

oranges

paints

police

Qq

queue

queen

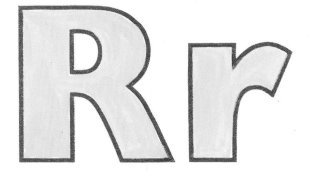

rabbit

ring

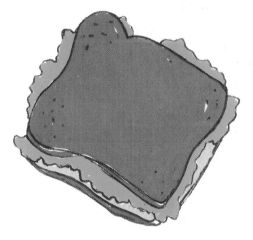

Ss

sandwich

sweets

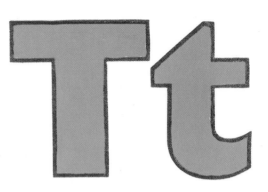

tree

telephone

unicorn

umbrella

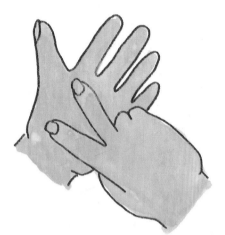

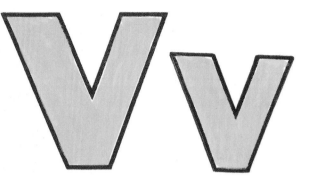

violin

van

FURNITURE
REMOVAL
VAN

watch

wheelbarrow

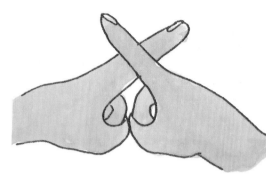 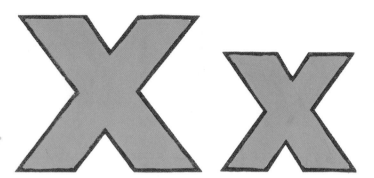

xylophone

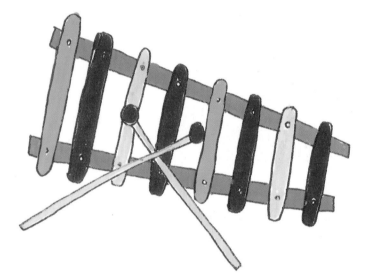

x-ray

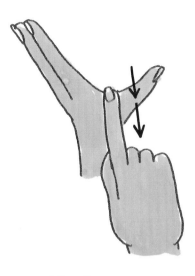

Yy

yellow

yacht

Zz

zebra

zip

NOTES

NOTES

PARENTS AND TEACHERS GUIDE TO THE SIGNS

AEROPLANE. Extend thumb and little finger, make ascending movement across chest.

APPLE. Jerk hand slightly forward and down, as if biting a crisp apple.

BOAT. Point hands as boat sailing.

BABY. Slightly rock the arms.

CAR. As if steering.

COW. Little fingers point up as cows horns.

DOG. Hands as paws for dog sitting up to beg.

DUCK. Open and shut fingers as quacking.

ELEPHANT. Move arm slightly as trunk swaying.

EGG. As if slicing top off boiled egg.

FISH. Flat hand as fish swimming.

FLOWERS. As if smelling the scent.

GIRL. Short single stroke down cheek.

GIRAFFE. Animal sign held high up, as long neck.

HOUSE. Bring hands down as roof of house.

HELICOPTER. Circle index finger, pointing upwards.

INDIAN. Hold two fingers at back of head as feathers.

ICE CREAM. Eating imaginary ice cream cone.

JELLY. Shake hands as jelly wobbling.

JUMPER. Closed hands from chest down to waist.

KING (QUEEN). Spread hand on top of head, indicating crown.

KEY. Turn imaginary key on palm of hand.

LITTLE. Thumb and index finger held slightly apart.

LARGE. Arms and hands spread right out.

MOUSE. Tip of finger twisted round in crease of nose.

MONKEY. Scratching movement under arms.

NUTS. Knock heel of hand twice on side of chin.

NECKLACE. Trace fall of necklace with forefingers.

OWL. Both hands make big eyes.

ORANGES. Squeeze hand at side of jaw, as if squeezing juice out of orange.

PAINTS. Use two fingers as paint brush, making imaginary brush strokes.

POLICEMAN. Move two fingers back, as if showing stripes on wrist band.

QUEUE. Left hand still, move right hand back in jerks.

QUEEN (KING). Spread hand on top of head, indicating crown.

RABBIT. Wiggle two fingers as ears.

RING. Indicate ring finger.

SANDWICH. Press both flat hands together.

SWEETS. Twist index finger on lips.

TREE. Slightly wave open hand.

TELEPHONE. Extend little finger and thumb as using phone.

UNICORN. Hand to forehead as unicorns horn.

UMBRELLA. As if putting umbrella up.

VIOLIN. Playing imaginary violin.

VAN. As if steering.

WATCH. Indicate watch on wrist.

WHEELBARROW. As if pushing the barrow.

XYLOPHONE. As if striking the notes on the xylophone.

X-RAY. 'X' hand, then both hands face each other from waist and above chest.

YELLOW. 'Y' hand, stroke down twice.

YACHT. Move hands forward as if sailing.

ZEBRA. Animal sign, spread fingers out on forearm as stripes.

ZIP. Hold one hand still at waist line, other as if pulling zip up.

ANIMAL SIGN. Little finger and index finger point up as ears
             middle fingers and thumb forward as face and jaw.

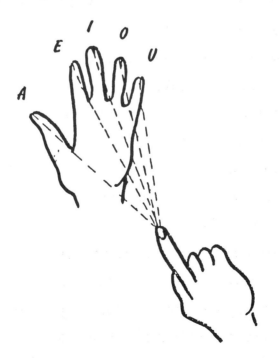

N.B. It is helpful to remember that the hand is used for the vowels.

ACKNOWLEDGEMENT

This book was made possible by the generous help of the following companies, trusts and individuals:

AIRFLOW COMMUNITY LTD .... High Wycombe, Bucks
BARKER, DEENA .... Sheffield
CANTOR, HAROLD   H & L CANTOR TRUST .... Sheffield
COLLINS, KAY .... Sheffield
CRABTREE, PATRICIA .... Sheffield
DRAKE, MARY AND FRANK .... Sheffield
EDUCATION SERVICES .... Oxford
GRAVES, J. G. CHARITABLE TRUST .... Sheffield
HARTLEY, JESSIE .... Sheffield
INNER WHEEL CLUB DISTRICT 127 (Ladies) .... Sheffield
LIONS CLUB, CITY OF SHEFFIELD .... Sheffield
MAY, FRED .... Sheffield
MARKS AND SPENCER, FARGATE .... Sheffield
MIDLAND BANK PLC .... Sheffield
RADLEY CHARITABLE TRUST .... Cambridge
RADIO SHEFFIELD CHARITABLE TRUST .... Sheffield
RAVENSCROFT FOUNDATION TRUST .... Gateshead
ROTARACT CLUB OF SHEFFIELD .... Sheffield
TALBOT TRUST .... Sheffield
T.S.B. BANK .... Sheffield
VINER RUBEN .... Sheffield
WARRINGTON, EDNA .... Sheffield
WESTFIELD HEALTH .... Sheffield
WINKS, MARY .... Sheffield
WOODCOCK TRAVEL .... Sheffield
WRIGHT, CHRISTINE and Lip Reading and Holiday Groups .... Sheffield
2nd Edition
YORKSHIRE TELEVISION .... York
SHEFFIELD DEAF AWARENESS SCHEME .... Sheffield
SOUTH YORKSHIRE FOUNDATION .... Sheffield
BBC CHILDREN IN NEED .... London
THE ROYAL MAIL .... Sheffield
HARROLD FOL .... Sheffield

A special thanks goes to all the staff and committee of the Deaf Advice Service Sheffield for their kind advice, sponsorship and assistance.

ISBN 0 9516851 0 4   Learning Together:
                          A Fingerspelling Alphabet with signs for Deaf and Hearing Children.
                          1st Edition, May 1990
                          2nd Edition, October 1990
                          3rd Edition, August 1995